The Crooked Mirror

Stephen Evans

"I just tell 'em. I don't explain 'em."

Eugene D. Evans, Sr.

This is a work of poetic fiction. The names, characters, places, and incidents are either the products of the author's imagination or are used fictitiously, and any resemblance to actual persons living or dead, business establishments, events, or locales is entirely coincidental.

Publisher's Note: Many of these poems were previous published in *A Look from Winter* (2021).

The Crooked Mirror/ Stephen Evans —First edition

ISBN: 978-1-953725-50-9

Contents

Foreword

So here's what I think.

A poem is a linguistic unity. It has no narrative flow. It has no time, no tempo, no pauses. It is the opposite of music.

A poem coalesces in the mind as the last element is read or heard; only then does it exist, like a quantum state collapsing into reality from the interaction of a reader.

The text of a poem is a single word broken up into elements. It is a delivery mechanism, and a flawed one. But it's what we have. And it is precious. Because a poem is as close as we can get to truth, given the undeveloped state of our languages. And minds, for that matter.

Poetry is where we're going.

At least I hope so.

STEPHEN EVANS

First Song

To that which moves, to that which moves, to
that
    Which penetrates the universal shine
    and shimmy, Roundabout, where other isn't

Within, without, non-centric circle thing,
    all light that which in most the light begins
    nor knows, nor can, who descent;

Because in drawing near to what is dear
    Our swallowy mind perspires and jealous
folds
    into itself where memory cannot go.

Truly whatever the realm holistic
    powerful treasures, body and mind, mind
    of which I thee sing.

Apollo, creed of the living
    vessel me in thy talented power
    bower of joy and sound!

One sum, it adds up to nought,
    for me, for you, for both
    swim to the center and cry.

If you can imagine, you, and breathe
    In deepest drawing scent
    While I watch in awe and innocence.

Ten cents a dance, the best
    That I can do, shadow of the realm
    Stamped in my brain, blessed, so what.

Once there was a tree and a crown
    Underneath it all and nevertheless leaves,
    Which shall you choose, O!

So seldom, Father, so seldom, do we,
    But we try, we have to try and
    of human inspiration can we?

So back to the leaves and so forth,
    They fall all over the crown,
    Where is it I say? I say

But no one answers. Maybe better voices,
    better voices after me, after me
    Alleluia. Please respond!

Just a man. Just a man.
    Wot! Spring me up. The silly lamp,
    Sorry a bit dizzy now.

Four courses and a better star
    That's the ticket, eh? Sir may I
    Rejoin the company next week?

So it goes, and as it goes,
    The lamppost lit, the sun did sit
    Blinked I in utter disbelief

When she left-handed once around
    Grasped and made a meal of it
    Like an eagle's wriggling trout

Second verse same as the first
    Jump and jamble in the ramble,
    Anywho to anywhere,

Look inward, chum, and verily buss you
    Buss you very much,
    And then maybe envisitation

Lures you to the place where it
    Becomes you in the you you then become
    Human all too human in the bones.

Hang around but try not so to hang
    Okay to sparkle just a little
    Around the misty edges, that's okay;

And suddenly last summer will be now
    And now the never will be
    Had with another sun the heaven adorned.

She looked and eye at her
    became bloved btrothed
    Bwildering a flashy pan

Who wouldn't even him must have
    With a god spaghetti sauce
    And such a rim revealed

So to speak of so and SOS
    Just so you know it was
    Him for whom and graceful flow

If a word I never use
    But if I did then if you did,
    Well, obviously!

Back to our story
    Our hero Harms no soul
    That Money does not modulate

Where's my umbrella?
   Parasol? By any other name
   Will block enkindled

New ewness of the light
   And airy penetration
   Never before with such a cuteness;

Till she, who saw me as I saw myself,
   To quiet my perverted my,
   Opened her mouth, as I did ask,

And she began: "If only if only.
   Stop chasing cars, thou dog,
   And stop and open and engage.

With where you're at;
   Good lighting of course,
   And not without with out."

By truth or consequence
   In essence and by quiet,
   Times before the crackling fire;

Rest content, but open and engaged
   Just don't look down
   The fire has lifted us.

I'm trying to help here,
    But I'm not your mother,
    I'm just another other;

But please know this: "All things
    Have order among themselves, and this is
form,
    That makes the universe resemble God."

Who is first sembled, always,
    In the end assembled
    As we must apparently.

Now now. There there
    In the beginning and so forth
    An origin story More or less;

Encumbered by the Heaviside Layer
    As the poet says, but what about
    The dogs; Oh I'm offtrack.

As universal instantiation delegates;
    This is in mortal hearts the motive power
    Kumbaya and so forth.

Boo hoo. Rah rah and other
    Exclamations of despair,
    And elegant intelligence, and Love.

Two Sparrows

Two sparrows live in the plastic tree
in the midcourt of the mall,
near the faux marble waterfall
under the plexidome sky.
I whisper: At least you can fly.
I'll distract them. Save yourselves. Flee!

Amanda's Chaos

Doubt, no doubt,
Her initial condition,
A sensitive dependence.

STEPHEN EVANS

Rain Forest

A spell of rain,
A loft,
A fire,
We entwine and intercede,
Grown close in lush anticipation.

Enlightenment

Siddhartha sat under
the Body tree
and fell in love
with you.

STEPHEN EVANS

What I Just Remembered

Sparrows argued,
Outside, early evening.
We said nothing.

A Passing Thought

For what is Lost,
a passing thought,
For what is lost is passing
and what is passing lost.

STEPHEN EVANS

Hope

Hope is a tree with red leaves
That linger at the top
And waver in the winter wind
And never wish to drop

Touching You

The trouble with smoke
(Crystal sometimes, sometimes
smoke you seem,
rejoicing in ineffability),
it never seems to rest;
while crystal is so very delicate.

STEPHEN EVANS

When You Are Gone

When you are gone,
I'm thrilled and disappointed by
every passing car.

Still Life

Still life.
Still unravished.
Still depleted.
Still unvarnished.
Still heated to the juice.
Still Life.

STEPHEN EVANS

Still

The falling leaf rushes
to greet its shadow.
Still, the shadow hopes.

Nine Eleven

They are still.
Still.
They are still.

STEPHEN EVANS

Spring (Finally)

Forsythia explode,
Fireworks frozen in flight.
Trees are more circumspect,
Understanding shade.

Forest Fire

Seek the path
Of vital devastation.
In the white pines,
Spring Forward.

STEPHEN EVANS

Crooked

Life is the crooked mirror
of the heart.
Not broken.
Crooked. Tilted
to show
what almost is
desired.

STEPHEN EVANS

Special Friends

In a love way,
knowing a flesh wound
narrows the gap,
will you yes you will
nights of dreams unmade
and mirrored days
flash and fade.
A splash across your face,
and drops retrace
the passage of the blade.

STEPHEN EVANS

Francesca

The wonder of your beauty
hasn't left me yet.
An ordinary dream
would have passed by now,
but here I sit, breathless,
unable to move, or think,
of anything but you.
It isn't fair, you know;

When I erect so delicate
a tower of enticing dreams
to shield me from reality
and all the world's petty cares,
and you, shaking your head
my way, dash, crumple
into clay, my mystic palace,
in one swift matchless glance.

STEPHEN EVANS

The Happy Couple

They see only each other. Speak alone.
He works, comes home to her.
She waits at home for him.
The neighbors barely glance as they ride by.

But the gravity of their happiness
speeds the Rising Sun.

STEPHEN EVANS

Subjunctive

I am not the love of your life.
You are not the love of mine.
But they are gone and we are here
And we shall love as if.

As if I were a young man.
As if there were more time.
As if the heart could shelter
Us from the failing hand.

Maybe it can. Maybe it can.
Maybe if I held you
As if I were your life's love,
As if you were mine.

STEPHEN EVANS

In Twenty Years

I won't recognize you
    But I will love you.
I won't recall your name
    But your face will bring me joy.
I will ask you what my name is
    Because I am sure you will know.
I will call out for you
    As you hold my hand.
My heart will beat faster.
    I will not know why.
But you will.

STEPHEN EVANS

Echo

Where in the breath of you
    Is there a sigh for me?
Where in the sun of you
    Is my eye's gleam?
I search for signs like hieroglyphs
    In the pictures of your
Body's twists and turns,
    In the winds of your mind.
I hear only the echo
    Of your heart's flood
In my empty chambers.
    But in the echo, music is reborn.

STEPHEN EVANS

Whispers

My pen can speak
the language of the heart
better than I.
It rolls along unselflessly
not impeded nor impulsed
by any thought of me.

As my heart flutters, so my pen.
As it flies, so speeds,
As it dies, so ends
and begins again.

I sit up high
and rationalize,
straining to taste,
to glimpse, to trace,
the unknown whispers
in unspoken lines.

STEPHEN EVANS

After the Flood

The barricades lay outside our content
and all the restless harrowing detail
of innocence was washed clean
in the blood of their falling.

We never chose innocence.
We never sought it out.
It is the consequence of barricades.

The deluge reveals buried treasure
sparkling in the amber moon
of the Restoration.
The eyes blink and are bold
with newborn sight
and tales are told
of Lost and Found delight.

STEPHEN EVANS

The City of No

In the maul of Ihknaton,
Wending the great hypostle pall,
The bearded prince in blind pursuit
Hunts revelations now irresolute.

Where mushroom-jeweled Seti rations
Judgement on the hypaethral,
The fabled adversaries pause,
While She bears youth within her fluent jaws.

The long suspended confrontation
Consecrates the ancient thrall.
"The answer was Man."
                          "It was", from the Beast,
As She slouches to the inevitable Feast.

STEPHEN EVANS

Rejoin

Rejoin the force.
Incite to riot
the condescending night
and mumble in your sweetest dreams
of time and twist
and the everlasting pertinence.

Wander in the West End.
Seed your way to freedom from?
Mercy? Thought? Dismay?

But no—
slice yourself though
the iron gates
and pierced and hollow
join again,
bloodless and whole and invulnerable.

Then let them attack.
Turn out. Turn in.
They'll never find you.

Like an accordion of the spheres,
you are not—
but listen to the sharp white whistle
of the bones,
the merriment of Pan, and Pandora,
sings again.

Somewhere in the Heart
the Messenger

Somewhere in the heart
the Messenger
Maintains the signal fire
and in the night
from smoke-filled chambers
emptied out of blood
desire jealousy and fear
feeds the embers
what is left of hope.
The fire burns.
The fire burns.
The fire.

Stephen Evans

When in the Night

When in the night the angels come
    And take you to some further place
Will you remember all the ones
    Who will remember you?

Or will you then forgetfully
    Pass on to other life and love
And time and breath and touch and reach
    And never more recall

Me? For I will not forget,
    Nor pass to other life nor love
Not time nor breath, not touch nor reach,
    And I will not forgive

The angels who have silently
    Or distantly or passively
Or mindlessly or recklessly
    Stolen off with love.

S<small>TEPHEN</small> E<small>VANS</small>

For Poor Vincent

I don't think men know much of poetry.
Women have the Gift, because the heart
is closer to the breath in smaller frames.
My own heart never rests. Funny thing.

We ruin with our pulse of Entropy,
new, clear fusion of close, fitting parts,
impaled at the fun end of the games.
I hear it breaking now. A Hollow ring.

Weave with me they say a tapestry,
target for the sharp end of the dart.
Endless empathy ends less the same.
Crack and crumble and begin to sing.

It never ends that never can begin.
Underneath the grief suppress a grin.

STEPHEN EVANS

Irresolution

On Bended nights, when resolution drums
Succumb, the eyelids fade and love's unmade
the bed that once you left, so red, all thumbs,
as I fumble the cap or wrap or strap or blade
of faintly rosy Marmalade (Oh yes,
I am Fructified, Crucified, Ossified, Flossified, until
Demeroled, Folderoled, Willeroled, Nilleroled, unless
Angels appearing to write in my hearing my Will
of the Wisp on a Stilly Nacht like this because
we often pause, toot sweet the falling reign,
enthralled at last, exhilarating flaws,
Devoutest wishes of the Saint of Pain
and Dreaming) often I dream of the Consummate You,
Irresolving the thaw of the Melancholy Dew

STEPHEN EVANS

In the Grass

The radiance, I'll give you that.
Nothing I know can bring it back.
Nothing I know. But what is that?
What do I know? I take it back.

From my sight, that is the key
To sing in, if you'll pardon me
For using such a word as key
In reference to this side of me.

Glory. There's a noisy word
For something best unsaid, unheard,
and Splendor, there's another word
that resonates, yet still, unheard.

Since nothing can bring back the hour,
Then nothing will bring back the hour.

STEPHEN EVANS

At Long Last

When I awake from this long sleep
　　what shall my eyes behold?
My pillow is a willow wreath,
　　my bed a slab of stone.
The willow dips to greet the morn
　　And glistens now with glee,
The stone the rising sun ignores,
　　immobile yet at peace.
The sculptor when he fashioned me
　　could never reach my heart.
Why then do I feel it beat?
　　Slow is the hour of art.

STEPHEN EVANS

She

She is all herself, and all of me,
    and all our lives unfold as she unfolds
and folds again, the passing of the rose
    into a state of lush serenity
and back into volcanic mystery,
    not knowing what she ultimately knows
but is, and is awake, and in repose,
    and in her pagan blush virginity,
and in her monstrous maelstrom gravity,
    and in her lucid night and foggy doze,
Aphrodite and Persephone arose
    and loved as one. A morphant synergy
of everything that opens and is closed,
    She is all, herself, and, all of me.

STEPHEN EVANS

The Possession

What do you do with it all day,
standing in the grocery line,
laughing in the theater,
walking in the rain?

Does it dangle carelessly on a chain?
Do you set it carefully with your keys?
Of the thumping, murmuring, jealous noise,
do the neighbors complain?

What do you do with it at night?
In your secret, sacred moment,
when you hold it in the candlelight,
do you know it beats alone for the joy of you?

STEPHEN EVANS

Making Room

Somewhere in me, Something hides,
making women love me not enough.
The scalpel elevates the skin,
a crimson imperative. The quest is on.
Something too cold, too odd, too old,
someplace the blood won't flow.

One by one, I slice and lay them
slippery on the floor. I hum
A tune: Kidney, lung, liver, heart.
Soon, oh soon, there will be room
for Love.

STEPHEN EVANS

A Look from Winter

The pressure of the promise we forget,
we old ones,
when we see the pale young ones
lying stricken on the floor.

We shake our heads for blighted springs.
We hoped for so much more for them than
this.

Have we not learned as they from watching us?
They know. They know. All things fail
that strive at all. There is no other life
than strife and blind descent from hope.

Yet something else we know:
There is beauty in the covering snow.

STEPHEN EVANS

Time of the Long Shadows

This is my time, a walk in the evening
when the sun is lost behind the trees,
when the sun is lost, and yet we see
still evidence of its passing.

The top-most branches filled with light
stolen from a parting source.
What they must have looked like in their day.
This is my time, when I'm at home abroad,

As strangers pass as shadows, nodding
In the stagnant glooming air.
The long shadows, gradually,
fading, drifting in to night.

STEPHEN EVANS

How to Mourn

We stopped the clock a week ago
while my brother slept on the couch.
The ticking kept him up.
I'm wearing my father's watch
But I can't hear it.

Friends have come and gone.
They didn't stay long
But we have lots of food.
I wish to remember
But it turns me sad
and I have work to do.

Here is my dream:
Skating in circles
on a frozen lake.
If it melts I drown.
If not I skate forever
Round and round.

For what shall I wish?
Pray tell.

STEPHEN EVANS

Closing the Beach

Roll up the ocean. Fold up the shore.
Sweep the sand into convenient piles.
10 P.M. Go home. The beach is closed.

Polish the dunes. Wave to the waves.
Unsalt the air and send the fishes home.
10 P.M. Go home. The beach is closed.

Mop up the marriage. Wring out the ring.
Sign the paper. Memorize the floor.
40 years. Go (pause). A life is closed.

Stephen Evans

In Black and White

In Black and White I let you go.
A silent movie plays.
Our Hero Declares:
I Never Loved You.

Valentino eyes whisper:
My Dark Unhappy Life
Is Not For You.

In Black he leaves her.
In White our Hero remembers.

PULL BACK. FADE OUT.

STEPHEN EVANS

Wind

This is the way it all winds down.
The empty chair. The silent town.
The slight relentless ritual.

This is the way it all winds up.
The after tone. The leaky cup.
The will to fill a listless hull.

This is the way it all winds in.
The fruitless race. The pointless pin.
The repetition of the skull.

This is the way it all winds out.
The whimpering stream. The ragged doubt.
The whine we never seem to mull.

This is the way it all winds through.
You after me. Me after you.
The unremitting canticle.

And yet there is the wind.
And yet there is the wind.
And yet there is the wind.
And yet there is the wind.

The Indivisible Rains

The indivisible rains
power the flood across the land,
coursing through myriad
uncharted, testimony
to the great seas,
the red sandy memory,
the verse resigned,
the night reclined,
the light refined.

Many the ways.
Many the wanderer.
All shall meet
the indivisible rains.

STEPHEN EVANS

On Brighton Beach

On Brighton Beach, the tourists say,
    the ice cream vendors come this way,
and come and go,
    and come and go,
on Brighton Beach,
    the tourists know.

On Brighton Beach, the bathers say,
    the shifting waves are quick and gay,
and come and go,
    and come and go,
On Brighton Beach,
    the bathers know.

On Brighton Beach, I've never heard
    the sleeping sand to say a word.
But come and go,
    and come and go,
the dreaming sand
    will never know.

STEPHEN EVANS

Monarch with a Broken Wing

Monarch with a broken wing,
    You will not reach the Gathering.
Your lover will not wait for you,
    But bandy with the chosen few.
No more to decorate the sky,
    A float of color passing by.
No more to augur Summer's end
    To one who speaks to you as Friend.
Monarch with a broken wing,
    Do not miss the gathering.
Gather lovers of your own.
    Dare to mount an earthly throne.

STEPHEN EVANS

Icarus

Squeezing through the tiny opening,
he slipped and crawled over the slimy rock,
stone whose surface never saw the moon
for all its nightmare curtain.

The lightless mist had held indifferent sway
for untold ages over water and lime,
occasional bats, blind jesters to the black,
and mushroom worshippers.

The child braved the silly dark
in tense pursuit of something,
(Rabbit or Mad Hatter—does it matter?)
One more step into the air,
and air was all was there.

STEPHEN EVANS

Time

'Twas twilight and he—
idle, on lengthening dark—
gazed to the fire (pyre) fire
which knelt before his form.

He turned and turned
the blade he chose
and chewed, turned
the lone companion
snuffling by the coat
and spoke—it's time—and left.

The coolness winding on his face,
he zipped and raced the shadow
'round the tree whose
apples once he hid,
a secret place, they didn't last,
wrinkled but still sweet
at summer's end.

C'mon we're late
he said and fled,
and followed close behind,
his shadow and his friend.

Me and My Shadow

Child of an age gone by,
He searches for lost Dragon tracks,
dragging through dust a rusty sword,
and shining his battered shield with lace,
a tattered trace of a Lady Fair,
who felt more like a carnival

to me: I follow him though
I'd follow anyone
who senses a direction.
I'm blind myself, can't hear a thing—
We walk and sing of Dragons
and his love.

STEPHEN EVANS

Whence the Rivers Come

A blind man groping,
fumbling, hoping,
Stumbling on a bit of light.

The way diverges,
surges, urges
On, no end but now in sight.

All lines now curving,
searching, swerving,
Melting finite we infer.

The circles ending,
bending, sending,
Mending now begins with her.

STEPHEN EVANS

In That Always

I am drawn to you, wondering why
We haven't met, and yet somehow I know.
Always there was you. Always, you.
Something deeper than mere déjà vu
(my best French, I know you know
I know you know it's true).
I somehow know the rhythm
of your breathing as you dream
(moonlit sable stirring),
your morning mood,
Your noon desire,
your sunset quietude.
I know you in that Always, where
I am drawn to you, beyond all why.

STEPHEN EVANS

A Chance Meeting

I met my dream on the road last night.
It smiled, dismounted, invited me to ride.
I shook my head. It looked surprised.

"I've grown too fond of my feet," I said,
"And your direction is the opposite of mine.
We belonged together once, I'm sure.
I'm pleased to meet you. Kindly step aside."

It was churlish, a bit, I know,
to something I wished to be.
But let my dreams find themselves.
Let me find me.

STEPHEN EVANS

Gently with Intent

A thought softly intrudes
on the fearful entropy
which consciousness exudes,
then slips into a dream,
Santa slapping your youthful face,
gently with intent:
Something finally
makes you stop and think.

In the fog you can't remember,
In the haze you can't regret,
there's a clarity that's searching
for the fisherman's net.

STEPHEN EVANS

Two in Times

In times aware of what you need,
you open to the cold and dare
the frost to penetrate, while
bold and trembling, slowly reach—
only to hear the note speed back
unanswered in the black.

In times unmindful, when you stare
unfocused on the life ahead,
you bump and laugh into a man
who dreams and is unshaken,
and awaken.

STEPHEN EVANS

Peanuts to Pigeons

Peanuts to pigeons
on a summer day;
but what I mean to say
is this—

Sugar to seals
swimming in a pool
(though they say
they like fish more).

Poetry is rhyme to run
the rhythm of the sea.
I am this
in the poem that is me.
Hopefully an epic,
But—we'll see.

STEPHEN EVANS

About the Author

Stephen Evans is a poet, playwright, and author.
Find him online at:

www.istephenevans.com/

www.facebook.com/iStephenEvans

www.gr8word.com

STEPHEN EVANS

Books by Stephen Evans

Fiction:

The Island of Always:
    The Marriage of True Minds
    Let Me Count the Ways
    My Winter World
The Marriage Gift
Paradox
Whose Beauty is Past Change
The Mind of a Writer and other Fables
Epigrammaticaon
The Next Joy and the Next

Non-Fiction:

Funny Thing Is: A Guide to Understanding Comedy
Prolegomena to Any Future Vacation
Layers of Life
Liebestraum
The Laughing String: Thoughts on Writing

Plays:

The Visitation Quartet:
    The Ghost Writer
    Monuments
    Tourists
    Spooky Action at a Distance

Experience	*Three plays about Ralph Waldo Emerson*
Generations	*(with Morey Norkin and Michael Gilles)*
As You Like It	*(by William Shakespeare, adapted by Stephen Evans)*
The Glass Door	*(An adaptation of Hedda Gabler by Henrik Ibsen)*

Verse:

Limerosity
Limerositus
Sonets from the Chesapeke
A Look from Winter

STEPHEN EVANS

STEPHEN EVANS

Milton Keynes UK
Ingram Content Group UK Ltd.
UKHW030149051224
452010UK00001B/28

9 781953 725509